PHOTO SCIENCE

SCIENCE 24/7

Animal Science

Car Science

Computer Science

Environmental Science

Fashion Science

Food Science

Health Science

Music Science

Photo Science

Sports Science

Travel Science

SCIENCE 24/7

PHOTO SCIENCE

JANE P. GARDNER

SCIENCE CONSULTANT:
RUSS LEWIN
SCIENCE AND MATH EDUCATOR

Mason Crest

Mason Crest
450 Parkway Drive, Suite D
Broomall, PA 19008
www.masoncrest.com

Series ISBN: 978-1-4222-3404-4
Hardback ISBN: 978-1-4222-3413-6
EBook ISBN: 978-1-4222-8497-1

First printing
1 3 5 7 9 8 6 4 2

Produced by Shoreline Publishing Group LLC
Santa Barbara, California
Editorial Director: James Buckley Jr.
Designer: Patty Kelley
www.shorelinepublishing.com
Cover photo: Dreamstime.com/Sam74100

Library of Congress Cataloging-in-Publication Data
Gardner, Jane P., author.
        Photo science / by Jane P. Gardner.
        pages cm. -- (Science 24/7)
        Audience: Ages 12+
        Audience: Grades 7 to 8
        Includes bibliographical references and index.
ISBN 978-1-4222-3413-6 (hardback) -- ISBN 978-1-4222-3404-4 (series) -- ISBN 978-1-4222-8497-1 (ebook) 1. Photography--Juvenile literature. I. Title.
 TR149.G37 2016
770--dc23
                            2015009817

IMPORTANT NOTICE
The science experiments, activities, and information described in this publication are for educational use only. The publisher is not responsible for any direct, indirect, incidental or consequential damages as a result of the uses or misuses of the techniques and information within.

Contents

KEY ICONS TO LOOK FOR

Words to Understand: These words with their easy-to-understand definitions will increase the reader's understanding of the text, while building vocabulary skills.

Sidebars: This boxed material within the main text allows readers to build knowledge, gain insights, explore possibilities, and broaden their perspectives by weaving together additional information to provide realistic and holistic perspectives.

Series Glossary of Key Terms: This back-of-the-book glossary contains terminology used throughout this series. Words found here increase the reader's ability to read and comprehend higher-level books and articles in this field.

INTRODUCTION

Science. Ugh! Is this the class you have to sit through in order to get to the cafeteria for lunch? Or, yeah! This is my favorite class! Whether you look forward to science or dread it, you can't escape it. Science is all around us all the time.

What do you think of when you think about science? People in lab coats peering anxiously through microscopes while scribbling notes? Giant telescopes scanning the universe for signs of life? Submersibles trolling the dark, cold, and lonely world of the deepest ocean? Yes, these are all science and things that scientists do to learn more about our planet, outer space, and the human body. But we are all scientists. Even you.

Science is about asking questions. Why do I have to eat my vegetables? Why does the sun set in the west? Why do cats purr and dogs bark? Why am I warmer when I wear a black jacket than when I wear a white one? These are all great questions. And these questions can be the start of something big . . . the start of scientific discovery.

1. **Observe:** Ask questions. What do you see in the world around you that you don't understand? What do you wish you knew more about? Remember, there is always more than one solution to a problem. This is the starting point for scientists—and it can be the starting point for you, too!

   Enrique took a slice of bread out of the package and discovered there was mold on it. "Again?" he complained. "This is the second time this all-natural bread I bought turned moldy before I could finish it. I wonder why."

2. **Research:** Find out what you can about the observation you have made. The more information you learn about your observation, the better you will understand which questions really need to be answered.

   Enrique researched the term "all-natural" as it applied to his bread. He discovered that it meant that no preservatives were used. Some breads contain preservatives, which are used to "maintain freshness." Enrique wondered if it was the lack of preservatives that was allowing his bread to grow mold.

3. **Predict:** Consider what might happen if you were to design an experiment based on your research. What do you think you would find?

   Enrique thought that maybe it was the lack of preservatives in his bread that was causing the mold. He predicted that bread containing preservatives would last longer than "all-natural" breads.

4. **Develop a Hypothesis:** A hypothesis is a possible answer or solution to a scientific problem. Sometimes, they are written as an "if-then" statement. For example, "If I get a good night's sleep, then I will do well on the test tomorrow." This is not a fact; there is no guarantee that the hypothesis is correct. But it is a statement that can be tested with an experiment. And then, if necessary, revised once the experiment has been done.

Enrique thinks that he knows what is going on. He figures that the preservatives in the bread are what keeps it from getting moldy. His working hypothesis is, "If bread contains preservatives, it will not grow mold." He is now ready to test his hypothesis.

5. **Design an Experiment:** An experiment is designed to test a hypothesis. It is important when designing an experiment to look at all the variables. Variables are the factors that will change in the experiment. Some variables will be independent—these won't change. Others are dependent and will change as the experiment progresses. A control is necessary, too. This is a constant throughout the experiment against which results can be compared.

Enrique plans his experiment. He chooses two slices of his bread, and two slices of the bread with preservatives. He uses a small kitchen scale to ensure that the slices are approximately the same weight. He places a slice of each on the windowsill where they will receive the same amount of sunlight. He places the other two slices in a dark cupboard. He checks on his bread every day for a week. He finds that his bread gets mold in both places while the bread with preservatives starts to grow a little mold in the sunshine but none in the cupboard.

6. **Revise the hypothesis:** Sometimes the result of your experiment will show that the original hypothesis is incorrect. That is okay! Science is all about taking risks, making mistakes, and learning from them. Rewriting a hypothesis after examining the data is what this is all about.

Enrique realized it may be more than the preservatives that prevents mold. Keeping the bread out of the sunlight and in a dark place will help preserve it, even without preservatives. He has decided to buy smaller quantities of bread now, and keep it in the cupboard.

This book has activities for you to try at the end of each chapter. They are meant to be fun, and teach you a little bit at the same time. Sometimes, you'll be asked to design your own experiment. Think back to Enrique's experience when you start designing your own. And remember—science is about being curious, being patient, and not being afraid of saying you made a mistake. There are always other experiments to be done!

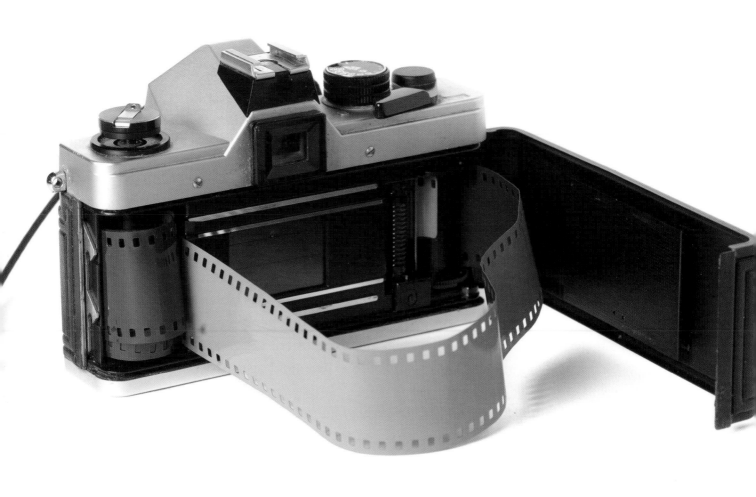

1
LENSES

Colin looked up as his little sister, Meredith, walked into the room. "What the heck is that?" she asked.

He looked down at the camera in his hands and the roll of film he was loading into it. It was an old 35mm camera, given to him by his father. "It's dad's old camera. He's letting me borrow it for my photography class at the community center."

Colin showed her the film he was loading into the back of the camera. "This is film," he said. "I use it in this camera to take pictures."

"Well, my cell phone and mom's digital camera doesn't need film," said Meredith.

"I know. That is new technology. This camera is old."

Meredith still looked confused. "I don't get it."

"Okay, let me tell you. A camera, even one like your cell phone camera, uses lenses. Lenses are used to focus the light and to make an image on this film."

"Lenses? As in contact lenses?" Meredith asked.

"Yeah," replied Colin. "Here, take a look at this." Colin showed her the removable lens

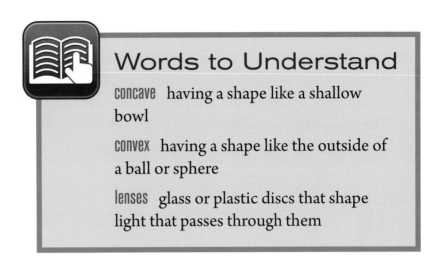

that he was going to attach to the camera. "Light waves are gathered by a lens. The shape of the lens focuses the light beams onto film in this camera."

"Okay, I'll ask it. What exactly is film? We don't use that in a digital camera or in my cell phone. Film is old," Meredith said.

"Yes, film is old. It's an older technology. Film is a thin sheet of plastic that is sensitive to light. The light energy that enters into the camera through the lens causes a chemical and physical change to the film. In other words, it is basically a permanent trace of the light that is captured in the split second the camera lens is open."

Meredith peered at the lens in Colin's hand. "Okay, then. How many lenses are there in that camera? You are about ready to put that one on it. Does this mean you can't take pictures without it?"

Colin nodded and said, "Sort of. You are right; you can't take a picture without a lens. That lets the light into the camera remember. The lens helps capture the moment the light enters into the camera on the film. But there is already a lens inside the camera. There are different types of lenses that you can add onto a camera. For example, one lens is a telephoto lens. These are often quite long. They have a long focal length which lets you take pictures from a distance."

"What's a focal length?" asked Meredith.

"It's one way to talk about a lens. It is a measurement of the distance from the point where the light rays come together to form an image on the film. This means that it tells us how much of a scene will show up in a picture. A longer focal length will have a narrower view of the scene."

Meredith said she understood. Then she asked, "So what other kinds of lenses can you use?"

"I was just ready to put this wide-angle lens on the camera," said Colin. "I wanted to take portraits of the dog. A wide-angle lens has a short focal length. It basically shrinks the scene in front of you."

Meredith dug her cell phone out of her pocket and looked at it. "What about the lens in this? I can't add new ones on to it like you can with that old camera."

"Actually you can add a new and different lens to a cell phone camera. There are kits you can buy that have wide-angle and telephoto lenses. They just are considerably smaller than these."

"I hate to admit it, Colin, but you seem to know a lot about this stuff," Meredith said, smiling.

"Gee, thanks. Never thought I'd hear you say that!"

Lenses

If you wear eyeglasses or contact lenses, then you are familiar with lenses and how they focus light and images. **Convex** lenses are used to correct some vision problems, such as with the contact lenses pictured, and are also found in magnifying glasses. **Concave** lenses are used in door peepholes to provide the person inside with a wide-angle view of the hallway. Concave and convex lenses are used together for other instruments including telescopes, binoculars, and cameras.

Try It Yourself

Imagine using a magnifying glass to make a picture. Impossible? Not so. All you need are a few simple materials and a dark room. Try this simple activity and see the power of lenses.

Materials:
- magnifying glass
- dark room
- sheet of white paper
- bright window or TV screen

1. This activity works best at night, or in a room that you can make dark.

2. Hold the white sheet of paper a couple of feet away from the light source (a lamp or a television). Have a partner hold the magnifying glass between the light and the paper.

3. When the lens is at just the right distance away from the paper, you'll see an image that the light source projects onto the paper.

4. If it doesn't work right away try moving the magnifying glass or the paper until you see the image.

5. What does it look like? What is this called?

**Careful! Don't try this using sunlight. The image of the sunlight on the paper could become very hot.

2
TAKING PICTURES

"Okay, so you have all these lenses in the camera," Meredith said to Colin. "But I saw you twisting the lens. Why did you do that?" Meredith was actually interested in her brother's photography lesson, but didn't quite want to admit it.

Colin smiled and spun a dial around the camera. "This dial makes the hole through which the light passes bigger or smaller. That changes the amount of light that comes into the camera in that split second that the shutter is open."

Meredith peered at the front of the lens. "So what exactly happens?"

"Let me show you." Colin spun the lens to its most open position.

"This opening is called an aperture," he said. "In this position, it is widest. It will let in the most light." He spun it again. "And this is the smallest aperture. It lets in the least amount of light."

Meredith shook her head and asked, "But what does opening and closing the aperture do?

Why does it matter how much light is let into the lens?"

"Well, think about it a second. If the aperture is wide, it lets in more light. It's good for close-ups."

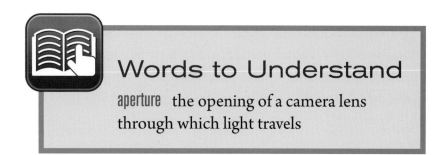

Words to Understand

aperture the opening of a camera lens through which light travels

"Oh, I see," Meredith interrupted. "But that isn't good if you are trying to get a picture of scenery or something. Too much of the picture will be out of focus. So in that case you would want to close the aperture, and let in less light."

Colin laughed. "See, you do get this stuff! And there is something else you have to keep in mind here. That's deciding what your shutter speed should be."

"Shutter speed?"

"Yeah. That is a measure of how long the shutter of the camera is open. The shutter lets light in through the lenses. Shutter speed is another way of thinking about exposure time. That is, how long the film is exposed to light."

"How long is the shutter typically open?" Meredith asked.

"Usually, a fast shutter speed—also known as a short exposure time—is somewhere around 1/1000 of a second."

Meredith stared at the camera. "You're kidding, right?"

"Nope," Colin said. "It's really that fast. But it could be open for several seconds if the photographer wanted. That would let in a lot of light, but also hurt the focus, because things in the picture might move. The longer the shutter is open, the more light hits the film. In fact, a slower shutter speed often gives a blurring effect to a picture."

Meredith sat back and looked at her brother. "I had no idea this was what you were doing in that class. There is so much to know. I thought taking a picture was easy."

The hole in the center of these lenses is the aperture, which can be made larger or smaller at the photographer's choosing.

"I know," Colin admitted. "I used to think so, too. Most cameras today are simplified. Cameras, especially digital cameras, can automatically do all this thinking for you—choosing the aperture and shutter speed automatically. That's why I really like learning about photography the old-fashioned way. It helps me understand the new technology even better."

Get a cool blurring effect by leaving the shutter open longer.

F-stop

The diameter, or distance across, the aperture is measured by an "f-number." You might see numbers written as f2.0, f2.8, or f22—the smaller the f-stop number, the wider the aperture. That is because the formula for this is:

f-number = focal length/diameter of aperture

When changing the f-number, it is important to realize that f-numbers are spaced one "f-stop" apart. By moving one f-stop you either double or halve the amount of light the aperture lets in. Phone cameras usually won't let you adjust this number, but full digital cameras often will. Experiment to find out how each f-stop move changes the pictures you take.

Try It Yourself

There are lenses inside your eye. When light enters the front of your eye, it passes through the cornea and the pupil. The pupil is the black spot in the center of your eye. Behind the pupil is the lens. The pupil can get smaller or bigger to let more light into the eye, just like Colin's camera. Watch this happen in this simple activity.

Materials:
- mirror
- light

1. This activity works well in a room that can be made light or dark. A bathroom works well. Turn the light on and look at yourself closely in the mirror. Notice how your pupils look.

2. Now, while you stare in the mirror, turn the light off. What happens to your pupils?

3. After a minute, turn the light on again. What happens to your pupils?

4. Why do you think the pupils change with the change of lighting?

3
IN THE DARKROOM

Colin caught up with his friend Piper on their way to photography class. "Aren't you excited about using the darkroom today? I've been waiting for it all week."

Piper looked less sure. "I'm not sure, Colin. Working with film in the darkroom is all about timing, and it's going to be so dark in there. I'm not sure how we'll be able to get everything done that we need to."

"Well, I think it will go okay. Miss Binn will be there to help," said Colin.

"I know," Piper said, "but this is it. If we mess up here, then the pictures we took this week will be gone forever. It's not like with digital cameras. These pictures are only on the film in this camera. I find the whole thing sort of stressful."

Colin laughed as they walked into the classroom. "You're just spoiled, that's all. This is part of what makes photography like this so exciting. It's the unknown."

Once all the students had arrived, Miss Binn reviewed once more the steps that they would need to take.

"The first thing we are going to do in the darkroom is remove your film from the film casing. You will be working in total darkness, remember, and will need to open the film case, load the film onto the spool, and then start the chemical processing."

The students took turns in the darkroom, loading their film onto the spools. They had to be very careful not to let the film drag on the ground. Miss Binn cautioned that touching the surface of the film with their fingers could leave spots on their pictures. "Hold the film on the very edges like this." She held up a strip of film in the proper way.

Miss Binn continued to remind students of the potentially dangerous things they would need to attempt in the darkroom. "You can touch the very end of the film strip, so this is where you will need to use the scissors to cut off the very end. Just work slowly, and use your fingers as a guide. Make sure you don't jab yourself with the tips of the scissors, of course."

Around her, some of the students seemed nervous. Miss Binn continued, "Then roll the film onto the reel, doing your best to keep your fingers off the film."

Piper raised her hand. "Miss Binn, this seems terribly stressful. I am afraid I'll mess up."

"Don't worry, Piper. If you mess up, you try again. It's not the end of the world. We have plenty of film, you can take more pictures."

Piper grumbled under her breath. "But I really like the ones I took, I think."

George Eastman

In 1888, George Eastman started the Kodak camera company. He wanted to make photography more accessible to more people. Prior to this, the equipment needed to take pictures was very expensive, very heavy, and very difficult to maneuver. The slogan of the company was "You press the button,  we do the rest." This meant that the customer sent their camera back to the company after the 100 pictures on the roll had been taken and the company developed the pictures for the customer. Their Brownie camera, introduced in 1900, sold for $1.00 and targeted the newest amateur photographers—kids!

Miss Binn smiled sympathetically and continued, "You place the reel into a canister like this one and close it up. Make sure that it is closed all the way. The film is now safe from light and you can begin the process of developing the film."

There was an audible sigh of relief from the students at this point.

"Now, we are going to be mixing chemicals here," explained Miss Binn. "Creating images with film uses chemistry, not electricity as in digital cameras. In a digital camera, the light is captured by a computer chip. With film, the light is captured by the chemicals on the film itself. Then we use other chemicals to make that image appear.

"Always use caution when using chemicals. One of the biggest obstacles is when you pour the chemicals into something else. Be very careful and try to minimize spilling and splashing."

Miss Binn showed the students the chemicals they would be using. "The steps are as follows: developer, stop bath, fixer, and then a series of water washes. The developer helps convert the image left on the film by the exposure to light into an image you can see. The stop bath ends the development process, so you don't end up with an overexposed or overdeveloped film. The fixer stabilizes the image on the film."

The film spool is placed in a container of chemicals to develop the film.

Miss Binn then let the students begin the process of developing their film. Along the way she reminded them that very similar steps would be taken when they went to print their images. There is another step to take from having the film to seeing a picture on paper. The film is a negative, or reversed, image. When it is printed onto film paper, the reversed image appears as a positive, that is, true to life.

"When we get to the printing stage," Miss Binn went on, "you will be using similar steps and chemicals. You will need a developer, and a fixer, and a stop bath then, too. And I promise, you will get some good images here!"

With that, the class turned off the lights . . . and got to work.

Try It Yourself!

Have you ever tried to put something together in total darkness? Working in a dark room, manipulating film, scissors, and reels takes practice and skill. What is it like to work in complete darkness? Find out with this simple activity.

Materials:
- windowless room or closet
- blindfold
- small wooden or wire puzzle
- paper, glue, blunt scissors

1. Put yourself in a dark, windowless room. If there are slivers of light coming in around the door, consider wearing a blindfold. The idea is to be in complete darkness.

2. It may take some getting used to, so be sure to stay still for a few minutes as your body adapts to this environment.

3. Using only your hands, work to disassemble and then assemble the puzzle. Or try making a paper airplane or even cutting and pasting together a paper chain.

4. What difficulties did you have? Repeat a few times. Does it get easier with practice? Do you think it would help if you tried to solve the puzzle in the light first?

4

TIME-LAPSE
PHOTOS

As the others worked on printing their photographs, Colin had a question for Miss Binn. "What exactly is time-lapse photography? I have seen a lot of videos and stuff on the Internet which shows a seed sprouting into a plant in a few seconds, or a baby growing into a teenager in just minutes."

Miss Binn pulled up a stool next to the workstation where Colin was and sat down. "You know, that is a very good question—and a very cool process.

"On a very basic level, time-lapse photography is a series of pictures taken from the same position that are put together in chronological order."

Colin thought a minute. "Yeah, that makes sense. You have to have them in order. You can't have the flower blooming before the stem grows."

"Exactly. If you wanted to work on this for your next assignment, I think that would be pretty neat. It'd be best to use a digital camera and some special software if you really want to do it right."

Colin said, "I can use my mom's digital camera. And I am sure I can find the right software on the Web."

"Great. Then I suggest starting small. Perhaps taking time-lapse of a basketball shot, or your dog running after a ball, or the sunset."

Over the next week, Colin set out to capture a time-lapse image of an intersection near his home. He decided to use his mother's digital camera. It was a **DSLR** camera and had a very rapid trigger. He could take a series of photos by just holding down the shutter button.

Miss Binn had suggested that he **stabilize** the camera. This would avoid any blurring of the images from an unintentional movement of the camera. Colin wanted his images to be very clear, so he borrowed a tripod from his father.

Words to Understand

chronological arranged in order of the passing of time

DSLR (digital single-lens reflex)—name for a type of camera that uses traditional lenses but captures light digitally

lapse a pause or short break in a series of actions

stabilize hold steady, keep from moving from one spot

Tripods come in many shapes and sizes.

It took Colin a while to decide what length of time should be used between the shots that he was taking. He knew he would be shooting pictures over a long period of time, and didn't want to end up with a bunch of useless shots. But he also wanted to make sure he captured the activity at the intersection.

"If I was trying to capture a time-lapse image of the sunrise, then it would not make sense to take twenty shots every second, for example. There would be so many images. But if I took one each minute, then it would work out," Colin thought to himself. "I think what I'll do here is take a picture every thirty seconds over the period of twenty minutes."

He set up the tripod and set the timer on the camera to take pictures at the intervals he had chosen. He stayed nearby the camera so that someone did not jostle it by accident. Time-lapse photography does not work if the camera moves even a fraction. If that happened, the images would not all match up exactly.

The following week, Colin showed Miss Binn his edited movie. "Wow," she said. "This is quite impressive, Colin. I wasn't sure if you were going to be able to pull it off, but you sure did!"

Time-lapse Microscopy

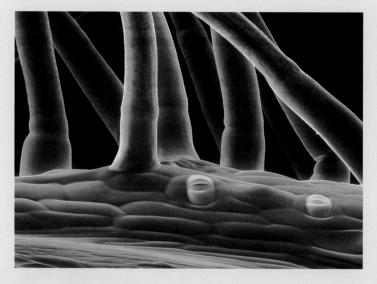

Time-lapse photography can be done at a very small scale. This is called time-lapse microscopy, which is taking time-lapse photographs under a microscope. This technique is often used in the field of cell biology. Because many cells are transparent and hard to capture with a camera, the cells are stained with a dye so that they are visible in the photographs. This mega-closeup of a thalania plant's skin was dyed green and yellow to make the parts easier to see.

Try It Yourself!

Time-lapse photography takes a series of still photos and strings them together in rapid succession to form a moving image. You could do that with a camera or you could make your own time lapse "movie" with a pen and notebook.

Materials:
- small pad of paper or notebook
- pencil and eraser

1. Decide on your "movie" theme. Are you going to draw a series of pictures to show two people racing, a cat jumping off a tree, or a skier jumping off a ramp and tumbling into the snow? The possibilities are endless. Start with a very simple scene with only one or two images in the scene. This will make it easier as you become used to the process.

2. Start with the very first scene. Draw the small image along one edge of the notebook.

3. On the next page, alter the scene or image ever so slightly. For example, you might want to have a character's arm move from his waist to over his head. Keep in mind that the smaller the changes, the more detailed your overall "movie" will be.

4. Continue until your scene is complete.

5. Hold the notebook by the spine and run your thumb along the edge of the paper to animate the scene—it's a flip book. Do you see it? Did you make a good "movie"?

Note: If you have access to a digital camera and a tripod, consider making your own time-lapse film like Colin did.

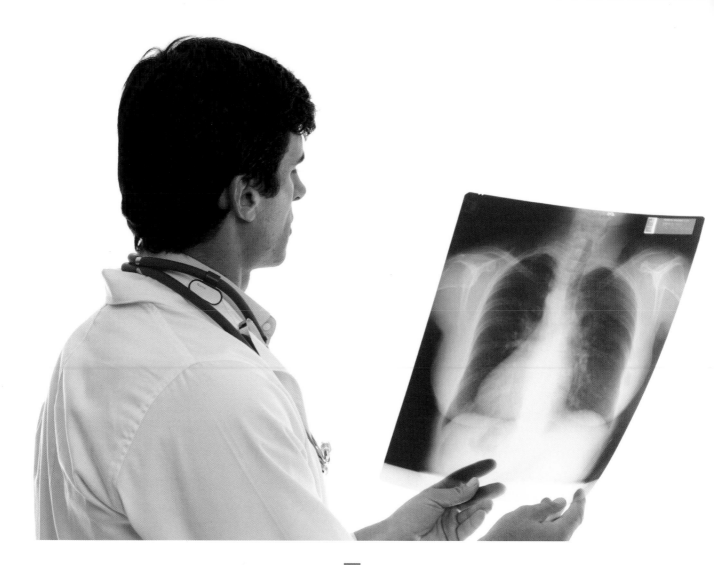

5
INTERNAL PICTURES

"We have some time while the chemicals settle," said Miss Binn. "Why don't we talk about some of the other types of photography you might be familiar with?" She started out by holding up an X-ray.

"This is actually an X-ray of an ancient mummy. An X-ray is basically a picture of the hard parts of your body."

"You mean, like bones and teeth?" asked Colin.

"Exactly. Those are very common things in the body that are viewed with X-rays. An X-ray is actually an electromagnetic wave. Have you all learned about that in school?"

One of the students chimed in. "Yes. We learned how electromagnetic waves all have different wavelengths and frequencies. Radio waves, microwaves, X-rays, and gamma rays are all part of the electromagnetic spectrum."

"Isn't visible light part of the electromagnetic spectrum, too?" a girl in the back spoke up.

Miss Binn nodded. "Yes it is. And don't forget about those ultraviolet rays from the sun! But back to X-rays. X-rays have a high frequency and a low wavelength. They carry a lot of energy and can pass through most objects, except for dense materials such as bones and teeth."

Words to Understand

claustrophobic unable to stand being closed up in a tight space

electromagnetic spectrum the range of magnetism that is created by an electrical current

electromagnetic wave a single part of the magnetism created by an electrical current

wavelength the distance between the tops of individual waves of light or electromagnetism

"Why does the dentist always cover me with a lead blanket when they take X-rays of my teeth?" Colin asked.

"X-rays also cannot go through lead. The lead blanket is to protect the organs inside your body. Too much exposure to X-rays can damage your cells and possibly cause cancer."

Miss Binn held up another image. "This is an MRI of a mummy. Do you know what is used to make these?"

"Magnets," said Colin, whose uncle had needed an MRI scan last year.

"That's exactly right," said Miss Binn. "MRI machines use magnets to scan the soft parts of your body. There are all sorts of uses. An MRI can find brain tumors, torn ligaments, or cancer cells. An MRI scan can also help diagnose multiple sclerosis or a stroke."

She held up a picture of a mummy inside an MRI machine. "An MRI scanner has giant magnets inside. The powerful magnet creates a strong, stable magnetic field. The magnets scan different parts of the body as the person moves past the scanner eye. A very powerful computer operates the whole thing and creates the scan."

Colin was still confused. "So how does a magnet make an image of your body?"

"It all comes down to the atoms in your body. These spin like tops, in different directions. When a person is put in the MRI, the magnetic field rearranges the atoms. About half of them align with the north pole of the magnet, and about half go with the south pole. But not all the atoms behave that way. Some are mismatched. Radio waves are then sent into the body to force

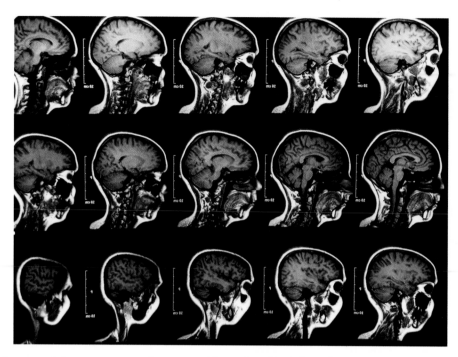

This series of images shows the individual visual "slices" of the interior of the body that are created by the MRI machine.

those mismatched atoms to spin the same way of those around them. The radio waves are shut off, and those rogue atoms spin back to their favored positions, and release energy when they do that. That energy is sent to the computer where it is converted to an image."

One of the students blurted out, "Whoa! That sounds like it would hurt!"

Miss Binn smiled and said, "Actually, it is completely painless. When patients have trouble it is because they feel claustrophobic in the tube. And it is very noisy in there, too. But there are actually no known hazards to human health when exposed to the magnets in an MRI."

Try it Yourself!

The atoms of your body rearrange themselves to align with the magnetic field in an MRI. What would that look like if we could see it happen? Let's find out!

Materials:
- bar magnet
- index card
- iron filings or small metal paper clips
- ziplock bag

1. Place the iron filings and the index card inside the bag and zip it closed. This will make the cleanup from this activity much easier.

2. Gently shake the bag on a table or desk so that the iron filings form a thin layer atop of the index card.

3. What does this look like? Make a drawing to illustrate it.

4. What do you think will happen if the bag of filings is carefully placed on top of the bar magnet? Make a drawing of what you think will happen.

5. Place the magnet on the table and carefully place the bag of filings on top of it. What happens?

6. Was your prediction correct? Draw what you see.

6
PICTURES
IN SPACE

"What do you think this is a photograph of?" Miss Binn held up a picture of a cloud of amazing colors against a dark background.

The answers came flying in from the classroom: "An underwater mountain?" "An anthill?" "A termite mound?"

Then Colin raised his hand amid the laughter. "I think it's from space," he said.

"That's right, Colin. This is an image of the Eagle Nebula taken with the Hubble Telescope."

"Wow! So there are cameras in space?" someone asked.

"Not exactly," Miss Binn explained. "This is not a picture like we know it here in this class. There are no cameras on the Hubble and no film."

"Then what is it?" asked another student.

"The Hubble Space Telescope, and other space probes, use a device called a charge-coupled device, or CCD. It records photons of light.

"Photons are very tiny particles of light. Really super small. All light is made up of photons. They don't have any mass, or weight. In fact, they travel at the speed of light, which is no surprise, really. Light moves at the speed of light, too.

"Photons actually make up all of the waves on the electromagnetic spectrum. Radio waves, microwaves, infrared waves, ultraviolet waves, X-rays, and gamma rays are all made up of these tiny photons. The telescopes on the Hubble and other deep space instruments capture the incoming photons of light from distant objects and record it on the CCD."

Colin had another thought. "I'm surprised that the colors in space are so bright," he said.

"Actually, the images that the Hubble captures are in black and white, not color," said Miss Binn. "Scientists use filters to determine the colors. They image the same object through different filters and combine the images to create what we see. A blue filter will show the blue light from the object, a red filter the red light, and so forth. Color can actually be used to make a detail on a distant object sharper. This is something that a regular camera image and our eyes can't do."

The original black-and-white image of Saturn from Hubble was colored by scientists using filters and info on lightwaves.

"Does the telescope and the CCD only record light?" asked another student.

"Great question," Miss Binn said. "No, it also records ultraviolet and infrared radiation. By gathering in all these different kinds of light, scientists can learn a lot about temperatures on these distant objects, as well as what they are made of."

She went on to tell them about the many discoveries Hubble and other space telescopes have found. The light in the pictures they capture has been traveling for millions of years. By seeing that light now, scientists can calculate back to when that light originated. That provides answers about the age of the objects they see in space. Because light travels at a set distance, they know how long it took those photons to reach Earth from their origin. Every visible object gives off that light. Hubble waits patiently to capture it as it streams by Earth.

Hubble Space Telescope

Since 1990, a massive "eye in the sky" has been bringing incredible visions of faraway worlds to Earth-bound scientists and space fans. The Hubble Space Telescope has orbited Earth more than three billion times since then and send back millions of images. Named for famed astronomer Edwin Hubble, the telescope is about the size of a large school bus and features a mirror for gathering those images that is nearly eight feet (2.3 m) across. It can gather light that has been traveling toward Earth almost since the universe began, more than 13 billion years ago. Astronomers have rewritten many of the things that they thought were true about our galaxy and our universe, based on the observations they have made with this revolutionary machine.

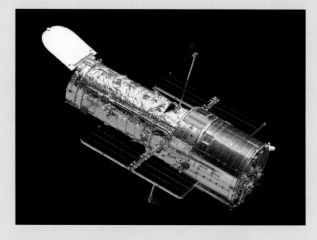

Try It Yourself!

Black-and-white images from space look very different from colorized versions. Scientists use colors to bring out some of the details that may be hidden in the black-and-white photos. What do you think? Can you make a picture "pop" using colors? Try this to find out.

Materials:
- page from a coloring book, two copies made on photo copier
- colored pencils
- regular pencil

This activity works very well with a coloring page from a hidden picture book or one with a complex geographic shape.

1. Color one of the coloring pages with only a black pencil. Experiment with different shadings of grey and black. Leave white spots in the design for emphasis. Be sure to only use shades of black or grey.

2. Now, color the same scene using the colored pencils. Use the color to highlight and emphasize the image.

3. What did you find? Which coloring shows more detail? Which is easier to see?

7
DIGITAL
TECHNOLOGY

Later in the second week of the class, Colin had a question for his teacher.

"Miss Binn, this has all been great. I've learned so much about photography, but it is more like the history of photography. We never really talked about digital cameras. And that is what most people use today."

Miss Binn smiled. "Colin, you took the words right out of my mouth. That is exactly what I had planned on talking about today. Because you are right, film cameras are rapidly becoming a thing of the past."

She turned to the rest of the class. "Don't get me wrong. Film cameras are still used, and in many cases produce very high-quality images. But digital cameras are what we most use now."

Miss Binn placed a small digital camera on the table next to her manual camera. "The film camera produces an image on film. We've seen this and now know how that all works. But a digital camera has to make an image that can be read by a computer."

Another student in the class raised her hand. "You mean it has to be in bits, and bytes, and pixels?"

"Yes. That is exactly right. Just like computer code—long strings of 1's and 0's that are used to tell the computer what the dots that make up the image look like."

"Those dots are the pixels, right?" asked Colin.

Miss Binn nodded. "Yes. Now, the basics of the two cameras are very similar—they both have lenses to focus the light. But the difference is where that light is focused. The digital camera focuses the image on a semiconductor, which then records the light electronically. That electronic information is read by a computer and turned into data. It is this data that can be manipulated into all the cool effects you can get with digital technology."

The students began to talk all at once. "Yeah, you can do all sorts of special effects." "And change the colors." "And the backgrounds." "You can even cut off someone's head and put it on to someone else's body!"

Look carefully and see if you can find the subtle way that this photo was digitally altered. (Not every photo "fix" is this easy to spot!)

Piper raised her hand with a question. "I have seen a lot of digital images that I think have been altered, but I'm not sure. Is there a way to know if something is real or not?"

Miss Binn shook her head. "Unfortunately, it is very difficult to know. It used to be that a careful look at an image could show some of the flaws. There might be strange shadings or random lines or something like that which would indicate that an image had been altered. But now, technology has advanced so much that it is difficult to know for sure if an image is real or not."

One of the other students in the class whistled under his breath. "You mean it is really hard to know if a picture I saw in a magazine is actually real?"

"Yes. And one of the things I hope you will do is to think about that every time you see a digital photograph. Perhaps that model wearing a new pair of boots doesn't really look like that, or maybe the sunset behind a new car is not real, and perhaps the picture of the surfer riding the wave had been altered to make the wave look very daunting. You never know."

Filters

Have you seen a truly amazing photograph on Instagram or on some other social media site? Turns out, that the photograph might not be as amazing as it might appear. Sites like Instagram allow the user to apply filters to their images. The filters can add or subtract color from a photo, a filter can be used to give a photo a vintage look by adding sepia or black and white to the image, and filters can enhance the color contrast to an image. All is not always what it appears in a photograph, and with digital technology it is easier than ever to make a good photo great!

Try It Yourself!

Most people have a big dream. Some people want to be a ballerina. Others would love to climb Mt. Everest or be a world-class chef. Do you want to scuba dive or fly into space or be a best-selling author? What if, with a click of a button and some fancy computer work, you could be? Try this and see what your future could hold.

Materials:
- digital camera
- photo editing software
- paper and printer access

1. Take several photographs of yourself. Include head shots, images of your whole body and some poses.

2. Use photo-editing software to manipulate the images. Can you insert your head over someone else's body? Can you put yourself into a space suit or on a beach in the Bahamas?

3. Use your imagination but try to make some of the photos realistic.

4. Invite your friends and family members to identify the real pictures and then the ones that have been manipulated. How did they do?

8
THE SCIENCE OF SELFIES

"Ugh. No matter what I do, I can't take a good selfie." Meredith slumped back in the chair, and tossed her cell phone on the table next to her.

Colin picked the phone up. "Here, show me what you've done so far."

She scrolled through the pictures she recently took. "My nose looks huge in this one. And I look like a monkey in this one—you can't see my ears. And I keep getting my arm in these shots. It's no use."

Colin chuckled. "Actually, there are ways to prevent all of those problems. I can help you if you want."

Meredith looked at him doubtfully. "Really? You can solve this? How do you know all this?"

"It's all about perspective actually," said Colin. "Here. Give me your phone." Colin pointed to the camera lens on the phone. "It's important to think about where you are taking the photo from. Most of the time we are just focused on what we are taking the picture of."

"Yeah, I'd agree with that," Meredith said sadly.

"The cameras in a cell phone, and just about any digital camera actually, have a wide-angle lens. This means that when you are pretty close—and by close I mean arm's length away—to the object you are taking a picture of, the view gets distorted. This means your nose looks big and your ears may seem to disappear into the sides of your head."

Meredith thought a second. "So the distance the camera lens is from my face isn't much different than the space between my ears. So this straight-on selfie thing isn't going to work, is it?"

Colin nodded and said, "Exactly. That is just what is going on. I did some reading recently and figured out some tips to taking a good selfie."

"Well," Meredith said impatiently, "are you going to share them?"

"I don't know. I know how much you don't like talking about science," Colin teased.

"What are you talking about?" Meredith protested. "This is taking a picture with a cell phone—how is it science?"

"Science is part of all of it. Physics teaches us about the properties of light, for instance, and lighting is important in photography. Natural light from the sun is better for photographs than artificial light created by electricity. Artificial light tends to create too many shadows and reflects off your face more, making the colors paler. If you can time your picture, try for early morning right after the sun rises or in the evening just before the sun sets. If that timing is not possible, stand next to the source of artificial light, not far away from it, and make sure you turn the flash off."

Photographers call sunset the "golden hour" for the gorgeous light.

"But what about my nose and my ears?" Meredith wanted to know. "How can I keep them from looking weird when I take a selfie?"

"One way is to get a tripod or a selfie stick which allows you to hold the cell phone further from your face," said Colin. " If you have one of those, then place it farther away from your face, and use the zoom feature to zoom in on your face. It will help make your face look more normal by narrowing how much the wide angle lens affects the picture."

"What if I don't have time to set up the tripod?"

"Then try to take the picture from an angle, rather than straight on. Taking the picture from a little above your head or from the side will help. In fact, it helps if you have the camera a little above where your eyes are. That's where we look the most flattering."

Meredith grabbed her camera and immediately started experimenting.

"Come here, Colin," she laughed. "It's time to do some scientific investigating!"

The Downside of Selfies

In 2013, the term "selfie" was the word of the year according to Oxford Dictionary. No one can deny that selfies are hugely popular and nearly everyone has posed for at least one. But many people have concerns about taking pictures of yourself and posting them online. Safety issues are concerning for parents, teachers, and others. People are worried about inappropriate and unauthorized postings of selfies. Young people posting selfies that are taken in ways that can be embarrassing can have consequences, too. Be careful when posting selfies. Don't open your pictures up to people you don't know. Always be respectful of others while posting pictures you might take of them. A good rule of thumb: Don't put up a picture you wouldn't show to your grandmother. If you can't post a positive comment about another photo, why not just keep it to yourself. Taking and posting selfies can be fun—but it is best to be safe while you do it.

Try It Yourself!

Can you take the perfect selfie? Colin had some very good suggestions in this chapter. See what you think and if you have any other suggestions that you can share with your friends and family.

Materials:
- cell phone camera
- tripod
- artificial and natural lighting

1. Take a series of selfies. Try to get good shots and bad. Use different lighting, different angles, and different backgrounds.

2. Share these with a few friends and family members.

3. Which do they like the best? What could you change to make them better? What common problems do you see?

9
CONCLUSION

Photography science—so many of us today are used to snapping a picture without thinking about it and then reviewing the image just taken on the screen. Digital cameras are truly amazing, but they are relatively new technology.

In 2003, it was predicted that 80 percent of the cameras sold would be digital by 2008. And that certainly came true; that number has gotten even higher since. Digital cameras are a part of our lives now, in everything from our cell phones to new technologies with cameras in a wristwatch. Technology has changed, but the techniques haven't really changed. As Colin and the other students in class learned, the concepts of lenses, aperture, and shutter speed still apply. It is just that in many of the modern cameras this work is automated for you.

Photography is not just for hobbyists and proud grandparents. Advances in digital technology have made significant changes to fields such as medicine, medical research,

astronomy, and archaeology. The ability to digitally image the human body, a distant galaxy, or the remains of an ancient civilization, and then be able to manipulate the images to see things in 3-D, or in color, or in motion, has contributed significantly to human knowledge. Those advances will only become greater with time.

For an additional activity, see if you can use a digital camera to record different kinds of scenes. Snapping selfies is one thing, but can you compose a beautiful image? Photography is so much more than simply pointing and clicking. The great photographers approached their work like a great artist. They thought carefully about the image before they took it. They studied how the light hit at different times of day or how the **composition** of the photo would change from different angles.

Try this using your digital camera. At your local library or bookstore, check out a book of photography. Look for photographic geniuses such as Ansel Adams, Galen Rowell, Charlie Waite, Margaret Bourke-White, Annie Leibovitz, or Nick Brandt. They all used the art of photography together with the science of photography to create the most powerful images. Take a

First step to becoming a photographer: Get a camera.
Second step: Open your eyes!

look at them. What feelings do they invoke? Read about their techniques and the science behind their photos. See how art can relate to science sometimes?

Now see if you can replicate some of the scenes, feelings, or ideas that they did. You might not be able to travel to Yosemite National Park as Adams did, but there is certainly something beautiful near you. You can't get Oscar-winning actors to pose for you as Leibovitz did (and still does), but with practice, you can make your friends into stars.

The idea that we can capture and preserve forever the images of what we see with our eyes is one of the most powerful combinations of art and science in the world. Imagine if we could have photos of King Henry VIII or George Washington or Socrates. Today, photographers are creating a record of our world—its people, places, events, and more—that will live for as long as there are people to look at the images.

Capture memories of a lifetime with your camera, like this image of London landmarks taken from the Millennium Wheel.

Photo Science 24–7: Concept Review

Chapter 1

Colin explains to his sister how lenses make a camera, as well as other devices, work.

Chapter 2

Taking a photograph requires knowledge of things like aperture and shutter speed; unless you have a camera that does it all for you.

Chapter 3

Developing black-and-white film in a darkroom requires skill, a little bit of luck, and some hazardous chemicals as Colin and his friends learned.

Chapter 4

Time-lapse images often are made from a series of chronologically arranged photographs. The results of this can be very interesting.

Chapter 5

Photographs are not just for vacations and school classes. This chapter covered some of the ways photographs can help doctors diagnose diseases.

Chapter 6

Photographic images are not just limited to Earth. This chapter explored pictures in space.

Chapter 7

Most of us have access to at least one type of digital camera. The benefits, and potential downfalls, of digital technology are covered in this chapter.

Chapter 8

Who hasn't taken a selfie? As Colin and his sister discover in this chapter, taking a good selfie is actually possible.

Find Out More

Books

Interested in black and white photography and the techniques to taking great pictures? Try this book.
Horenstein, Henry. *Black-and-White Photography: A Basic Manual.* New York: Little, Brown, and Company, 2004.

Want to know about the science behind photography? This book is a great place to start.
Johnson, Charles S. *Science for the Curious Photographer: An Introduction to the Science of Photography.* London: A K Peters/CRC Press, 2010.

Want to take better pictures? This is the place to start.
Miotke, Jim. *BetterPhoto Basics: The Absolute Beginner's Guide to Taking Photos Like a Pro.* North Mankota, Minn.: Amphoto Books, 2010.

Web Sites

Interested in photos from space? Check out these amazing images from space taken by the Hubble Space Craft.
www.spacetelescope.org/images/archive/top100/

This Web site has fascinating images from MRIs of the human body.
www.nlm.nih.gov/research/visible/mri.html

Want some more hints for taking that perfect selfie? Check this out.
www.wikihow.com/Take-Good-Selfies

Series Glossary of Key Terms

alleles   different forms of a gene; offspring inherit one allele from each parent

chromosomes   molecules within an organism which contain DNA

climate change   the ongoing process in which the temperature of the Earth is growing over time

force   in science, strength or energy that comes as a result of a physical movement or action

frequency   number of waves that pass a given point in a certain period of time

friction   the resistance encountered when an object rubs against another object or on a surface

gene   molecular unit of heredity of living organisms

gravity   the force that pulls objects toward the ground

greenhouse gases   gases in the atmosphere that trap radiation from the sun

inertia   tendency of an object to resist change in motion

laser   an intensified beam of light

lift   the force that acts to raise a wing or an airfoil

momentum   the amount of motion by a moving object

semiconductor a substance that has a conductivity between that of an insulator and that of most metals

sustainable   able to be maintained at a certain rate or level

traits   characteristics of an organism that are passed to the next generation

wavelength   a measurement of light that is the distance from the top of one wave to the next

Picture Credits

Ansel Adams/Department of the Interior: 40

Dreamstime.com: Andrew Buckin 8; Zhekos 10; Leungchopan 12; Empire331 13; Hxdylzj 14; CorepixVof 16; EllenMol1814 17; Valpal 18; Cesarechimenti 21; Hetipaves 22; Showface 24; Bunyos 26; Ogione 32; Kaspiic 33; THPStock 34; William87 36; Oneinchpunch 37; Khrozevshka 41; Ronscall 1

Shutterstock: Emilia Stasiak 20

NASA: Hubble/ESA: 28; Hubble Space Images: 29; 30.

ABOUT THE AUTHOR

Jane P. Gardner has written more than a dozen books for young and young-adult readers on science and other nonfiction topics. She became an author after a career as a science educator. She lives in Massachusetts with her husband, two sons, plus a cat and a gecko!

ABOUT THE CONSULTANT

Russ Lewin has taught physics, robotics, astronomy, and math at Santa Barbara Middle School in California for more than 25 years. His creative and popular classes and curriculum include a hands-on approach to learning and exploring that instills a love of science in his students.

INDEX